The Tree

BY DIANE'S HOUSE

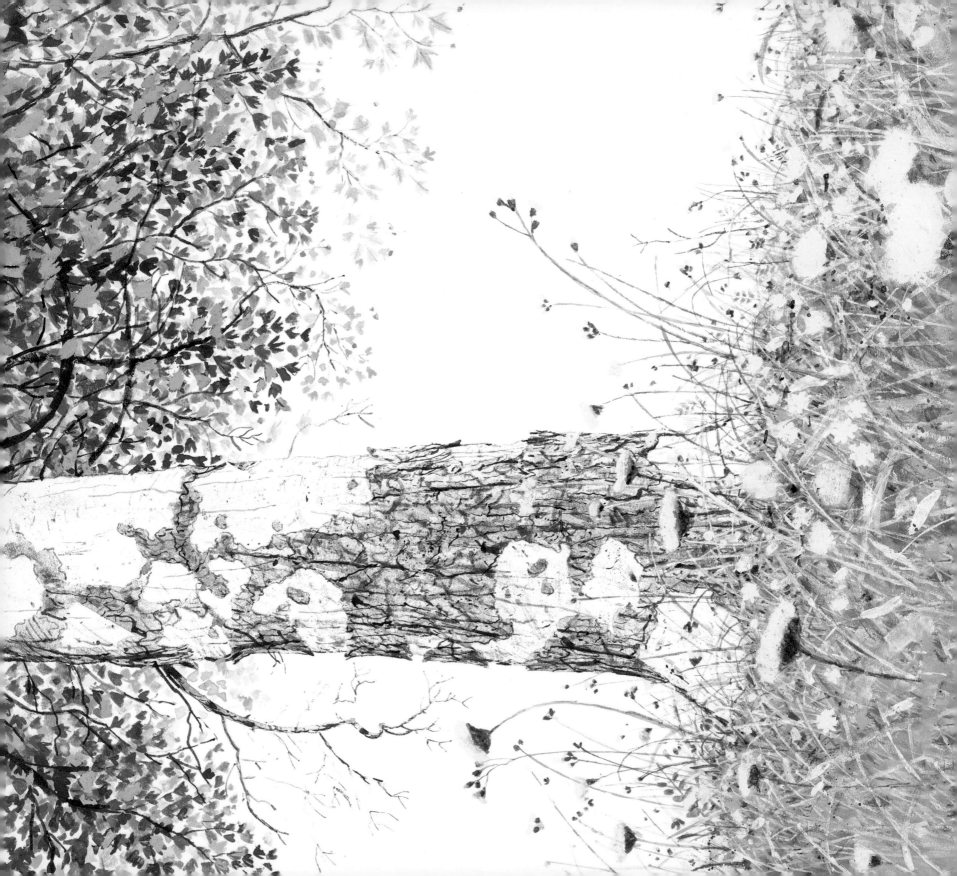

The Tree

BY DIANE'S HOUSE

I Wonder Why

By Lawrence F. Lowery

Illustrated by Tim and Gregg Hildebrandt

NSTA Kids
National Science Teachers Association
Arlington, Virginia

NSTA Kids
National Science Teachers Association ™

Claire Reinburg, Director
Wendy Rubin, Managing Editor
Andrew Cooke, Senior Editor
Amanda O'Brien, Associate Editor
Donna Yudkin, Book Acquisitions Coordinator

ART AND DESIGN
Will Thomas Jr., Director
Joseph Butera, Cover, Interior Design
Original illustrations by Tim and Gregg Hildebrandt

PRINTING AND PRODUCTION
Catherine Lorrain, Director

Lexile® measure: 630L

NATIONAL SCIENCE TEACHERS ASSOCIATION
David L. Evans, Executive Director
David Beacom, Publisher

1840 Wilson Blvd., Arlington, VA 22201
www.nsta.org/store
For customer service inquiries, please call 800-277-5300.

PERMISSIONS

Library of Congress Cataloging-in-Publication Data

Lowery, Lawrence F.
  The tree by Diane's house / by Lawrence F. Lowery.
     pages cm
  ISBN 978-1-941316-25-2
  1. Trees—Life cycles—Juvenile literature. 2. Trees—Ecology—Juvenile literature. I. Title.
  QK475.8.L69 2015
  582.16—dc23
                                              2015020089

Cataloging-in-Publication Data for the e-book are also available from the Library of Congress.
e-LCCN: 2015020740

Introduction

The *I Wonder Why* series is a set of science books created specifically for young learners who are in their first years of school. The content for each book was chosen to be appropriate for youngsters who are beginning to construct knowledge of the world around them. These youngsters ask questions. They want to know about things. These youngsters ask questions. They want to know about things. They are more curious than they will be when they are a decade older. Research shows that science is students' favorite subject when they enter school for the first time.

Science is both *what* we know and *how* we come to know it. What we know is the content knowledge that accumulates over time as scientists continue to explore the universe in which we live. How we come to know science is the set of thinking and reasoning processes we use to get answers to the questions and inquiries in which we are engaged.

Scientists learn by observing, comparing, and organizing the objects and ideas they are investigating. Children learn the same way. The thinking processes are among several inquiry behaviors that enable us to find out about our world and how it works. Observing, comparing, and organizing are fundamental to the more advanced thinking processes of relating, experimenting, and inferring.

The five books in this set of the *I Wonder Why* series focus on the biological sciences. Biology is the study of living things. It is such a large field of study that scientists have divided it into two parts: botany (the study of plants) and zoology (the study of animals). Each of those parts is then divided into many more fields of study.

These books introduce the reader to basic science content pertaining to plants and animals. The content includes the concepts of growth, life cycles, and food chains (*The Tree by Diane's House*); inferences derived by observing patterns in plant structures (*Our Very Own Tree*); factors needed for a healthy living environment (*Tommy's Turtle*); protective coloration and camouflage characteristics of animals (*Looking for Animals*); and comparisons of observable similarities and differences among animals (*Animals Two by Two*).

Each book uses a different approach to take the reader through simple scientific information. A couple of books are expository, providing factual information. A few are narratives that involve the reader in the discovery of the properties of living organisms. Another book uses cumulative rhythmic sentences to engage the reader in a form of literary growth that corresponds with the biological growth in the story. The combination of different literary ways to present information brings the content to the reader through several instructional avenues.

In addition, the content in these books supports the criteria set forth by the *Common Core State Standards*. Unlike didactic presentations of knowledge, the content is woven into each book so that its presence is subtle but powerful.

The science activities in the Parent/Teacher Handbook in each book enable learners to carry out their own investigations related to the content. The materials needed for these activities are easily obtained, and the activities have been tested with youngsters to be sure they are age appropriate.

After the reader completes a science activity, rereading or referring back to the book and talking about connections with the activity can be a deepening experience that stabilizes the learning as a long-term memory.

These are some seeds
that fell to the ground
and grew in the soil
near Diane's house.

This is a seedling, supple and slim,
that sprouted from a seed
that fell to the ground
and grew in the soil
near Diane's house.

This is the sapling, tall and thin,
that rose from the seedling, supple and slim,
that sprouted from a seed
that fell to the ground
and grew in the soil
near Diane's house.

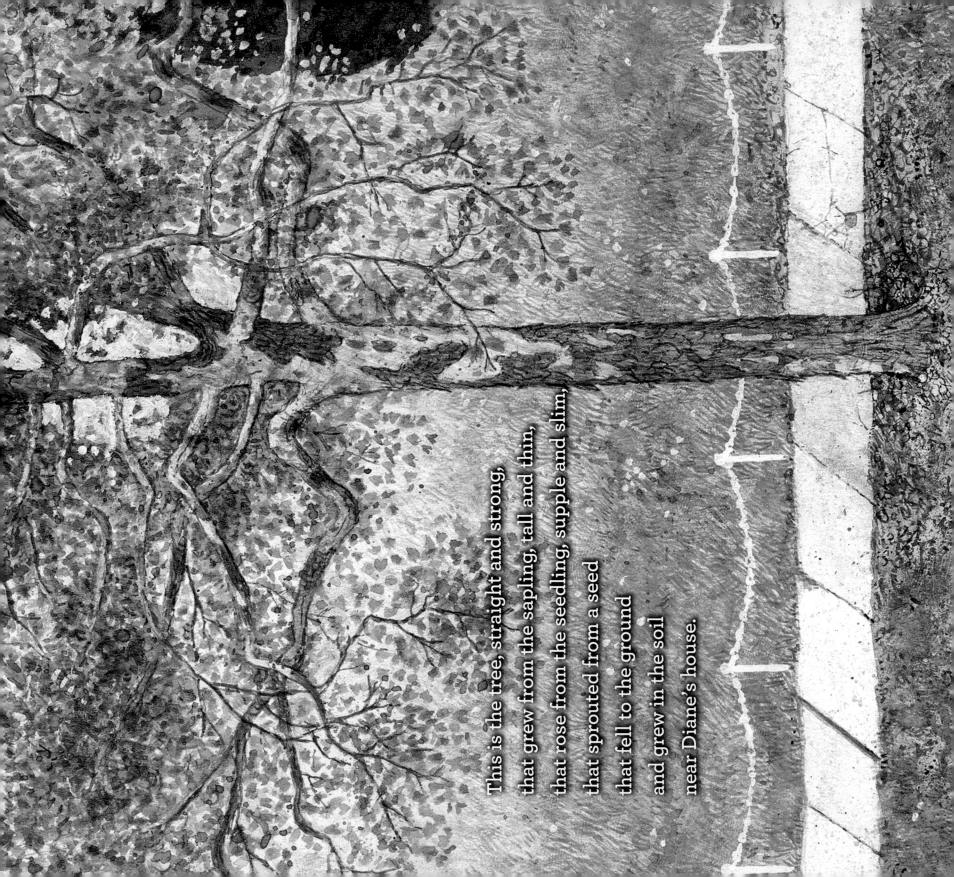

This is the tree, straight and strong,
that grew from the sapling, tall and thin,
that rose from the seedling, supple and slim,
that sprouted from a seed
that fell to the ground
and grew in the soil
near Diane's house.

These are the caterpillars, long and lean,

that chewed some leaves, jagged and green,
that covered the tree, straight and strong,
that grew from the sapling, tall and thin,
that rose from the seedling, supple and slim,
that sprouted from a seed
that fell to the ground
and grew in the soil
near Diane's house.

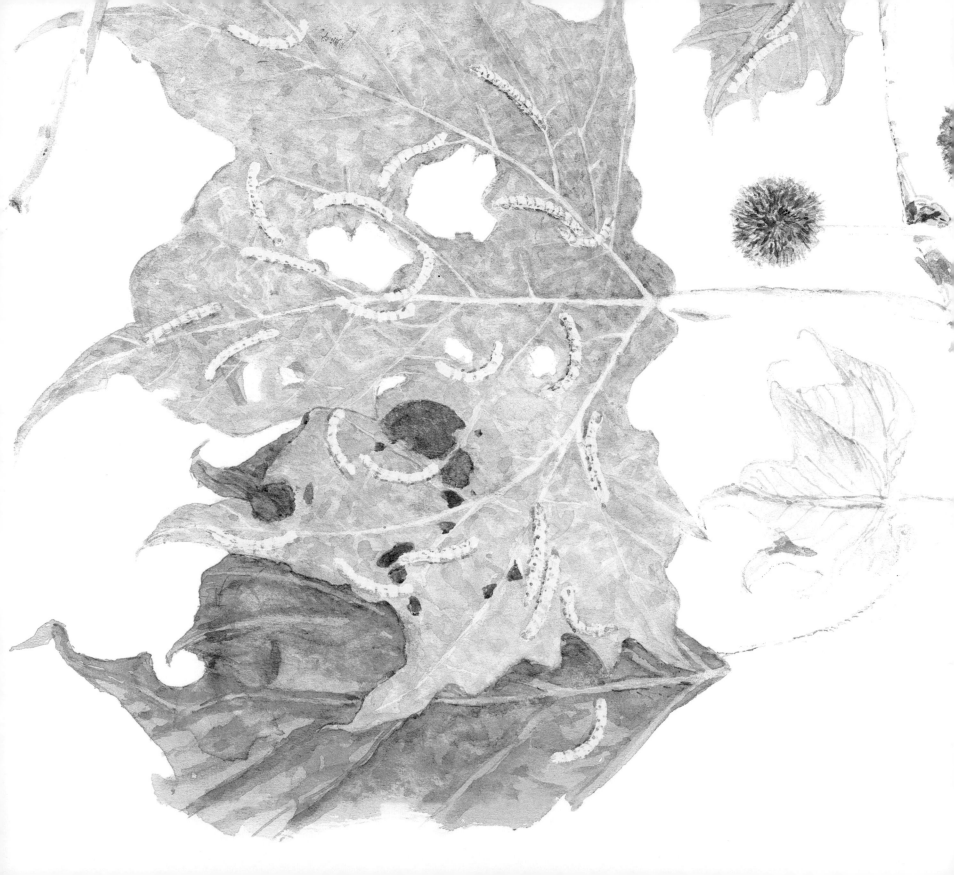

These are the birds, so easily seen,
that ate some caterpillars, long and lean,
that chewed some leaves, jagged and green,
that covered the tree, straight and strong,
that grew from the sapling, tall and thin,
that rose from the seedling, supple and slim,
that sprouted from a seed
that fell to the ground
and grew in the soil
near Diane's house.

This is the hawk, with eyes so keen,

that caught some birds, so easily seen,
that ate some caterpillars, long and lean,
that chewed some leaves, jagged and green,
that covered the tree, straight and strong,
that grew from the sapling, tall and thin,
that rose from the seedling, supple and slim,
that sprouted from a seed
that fell to the ground
and grew in the soil
near Diane's house.

This is the man with a very sharp saw.

He sawed down the tree, straight and strong,

that grew from the sapling, tall and thin,

that rose from the seedling, supple and slim,

that sprouted from a seed

that fell to the ground

and grew in the soil

near Diane's house.

Now the caterpillars, long and lean,
have no leaves to eat, so they go away.
Now the birds, so easily seen,
have no caterpillars to eat, so they go away.
Now the hawk, with eyes so keen,
has no birds to eat, so it goes away.

Now Diane's house looks sad and lonely.

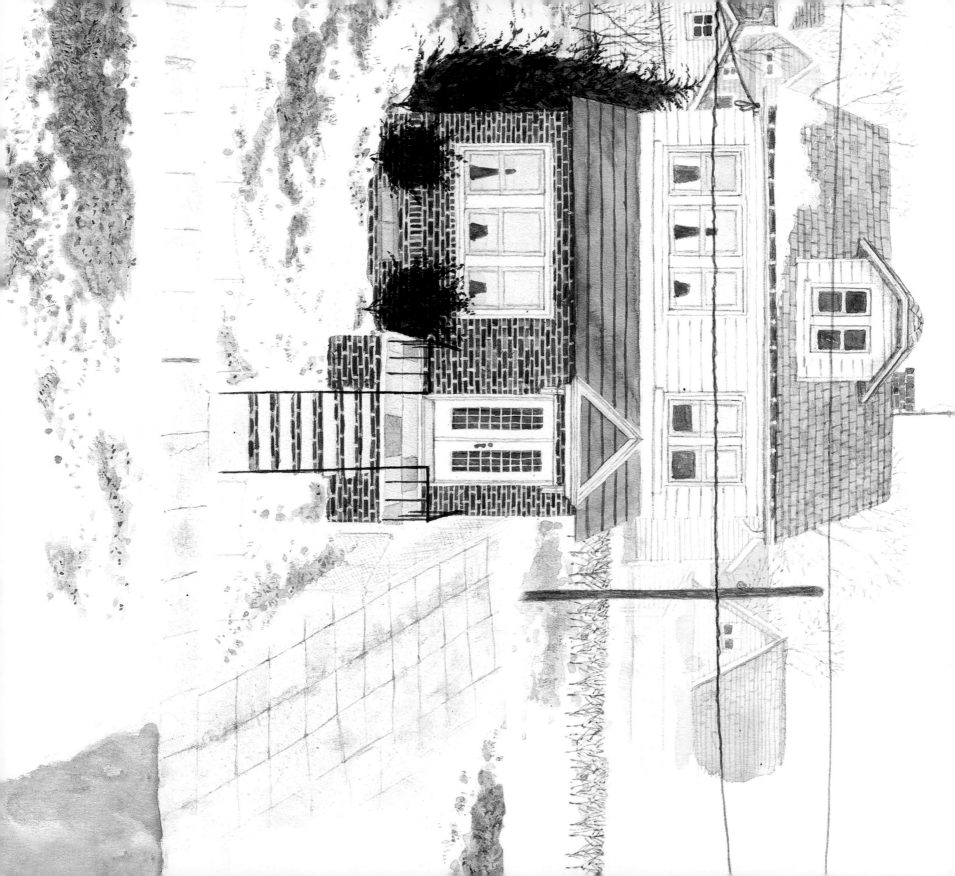

Parent/Teacher Handbook

The Tree

BY DIANE'S HOUSE

Introduction

The cycle of germination and growth of a tree from seed to tree, the interdependence of living things in nature, the food chain, the care of our environment, and aesthetics are the central ideas developed in *The Tree by Diane's House*. As Diane grows from childhood to her late teens, the tree grows from a seedling to a full, mature tree.

Inquiry Processes

No single process is emphasized in this book, but rather it focuses on the total interaction of many processes that are involved in the relationship between people and nature. The interdependence of people and nature is an aspect scientists must focus on continuously to properly evaluate the effect of their work.

Content

In this book, the germination and growth of a tree through its sequential stages from seed to seedling to sapling to mature tree to germination again depicts the life cycle of a plant—in this case, the life cycle of a sycamore tree.

The food chain between the plant and animals is depicted in the story. The cycle of the leaves, caterpillars, birds, and hawk illustrate how one animal is dependent on another animal for food and that all the animals depend on plants indirectly or directly.

The failure of humans to manage their environments thoughtfully is illustrated by the human disruption of the animal food chain in cutting down the tree. The aesthetics of the environment also are affected by the act: "Now Diane's house looks sad and lonely."

The writing in this book is cumulative, with each page adding a new part to the story to suggest a sense of growth over time in a literary way.

Science Activities

Survey Your Neighborhood

Survey your neighborhood to note ways people may be damaging the immediate environment. Has a construction builder removed too many trees to construct homes in a particular location? Are trees being planted in locations where they might cause problems in the future?

Observing How Fast Different Seeds Begin to Grow

In this story, both Diane and the tree by her home grow. In the plant world, some plants begin to grow faster than others. You can compare how fast some plants begin to grow by setting up an experiment.

You will need three flowerpots with saucers under them, labels, good planting soil, and three kinds of seeds (e.g., pea, squash, and sunflower). Fill pots with the same amount of potting soil in each. Plant five seeds of each plant in separate pots (e.g., five sunflower seeds in one pot, five pea seeds in another pot, and five squash seeds in a third pot). Label each pot with the name of the seed and the date the seeds were planted. Place each pot in its saucer, set the saucers in a place that gets sunlight, and keep the seeds watered.

Observe the pots each day, and record the date when the seeds sprout. Add other information, such as when leaves appear.

Write a report about the plants and describe the differences in rates of sprouting of the three kinds of seeds. Make a drawing of each of the plants for your report, and label the parts of the plants that you see. The following chart shows the approximate germination times for many common seeds. Test some of these seeds to see if what you find matches the times on the chart.

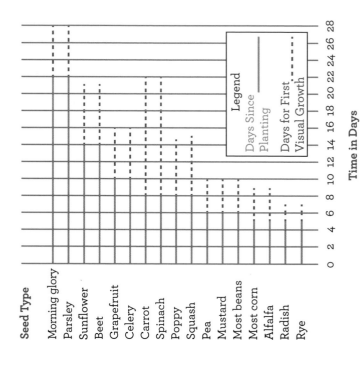

Approximate Germination Times for Common Seeds

Legend
Days Since Planting ——————
Days for First Visual Growth --------

Seed Type: Morning glory, Parsley, Sunflower, Beet, Grapefruit, Celery, Carrot, Spinach, Poppy, Squash, Pea, Mustard, Most beans, Most corn, Alfalfa, Radish, Rye

Time in Days: 0 2 4 6 8 10 12 14 16 18 20 22 24 26 28

Note: Most seeds will germinate over a wide temperature range. Generally, seeds take longer to germinate at low temperatures. The germination periods represented in this table are for a temperature range of 65°F–75°F (19°C–24°C).

Additional activities can be found at www.nsta.org/tree.